Great Americans
Chief Joseph

Barbara Kiely Miller

Reading consultant: Susan Nations, M.Ed., author/literacy coach/ consultant in literacy development

WEEKLY READER®
PUBLISHING

Please visit our web site at: **www.garethstevens.com**
For a free color catalog describing our list of high-quality books,
call 1-800-542-2595 (USA) or 1-800-387-3178 (Canada).

Library of Congress Cataloging-in-Publication Data

Kiely Miller, Barbara.
   Chief Joseph / by Barbara Kiely Miller.
     p. cm. — (Great Americans)
   Includes bibliographical references and index.
   ISBN-13: 978-0-8368-8314-5 (lib. bdg.)
   ISBN-13: 978-0-8368-8321-3 (softcover)
   ISBN-10: 0-8368-8314-4 (lib. bdg.)
   ISBN-10: 0-8368-8321-7 (softcover)
   1. Joseph, Nez Percé Chief, 1840-1904—Juvenile literature.
2. Nez Percé Indians—Kings and rulers—Biography—Juvenile
literature. 3. Nez Percé Indians—Wars, 1877—Juvenile literature.
I. Title.
   E99.N5J645   2008
   979.5004'9741240092—dc22   2007012093

This edition first published in 2008 by
Weekly Reader® Books
An imprint of Gareth Stevens Publishing
1 Reader's Digest Road
Pleasantville, NY 10570-7000 USA

Copyright © 2008 by Gareth Stevens, Inc.

Managing editor: Valerie J. Weber
Art direction: Tammy West
Cover design and page layout: Charlie Dahl
Picture research: Sabrina Crewe
Production: Jessica Yanke

Picture credits: Cover, title page The Granger Collection, New York; pp. 5, 7, 17, 20 Library of Congress; p. 6 Eric W. Valentine; pp. 9, 19 Washington State Historical Society, Tacoma; pp. 10, 14 Stefan Chabluk and Charlie Dahl/© Gareth Stevens, Inc.; p. 12 L94-7.105, Northwest Museum of Arts & Culture/Eastern Washington State Historical Society, Spokane, Washington; pp. 13, 16 photo courtesy of National Park Service, Nez Perce National Historical Park; p. 15 © North Wind Picture Archives; p. 21 © Bettmann/Corbis.

All rights reserved. No part of this book may be reproduced, stored in a retrieval system, or transmitted in any form or by any means, electronic, mechanical, photocopying, recording, or otherwise, without the prior written permission of the copyright holder.

Printed in the United States of America

1 2 3 4 5 6 7 8 9 11 10 09 08 07

Table of Contents

Chapter 1: Life Among the Nez Perce 4
Chapter 2: Making Friends and Enemies 8
Chapter 3: Leading His People 11
Chapter 4: A Statesman for the Nez Perce . . 18
Glossary 22
For More Information 23
Index 24

Cover and title page: Chief Joseph was a Nez Perce leader. He fought to keep his people's homeland and for the right of Native Americans to have the same laws and freedoms as other people.

Chapter 1

Life Among the Nez Perce

Chief Joseph had led the Nez Perce Indians 1,500 miles (2,400 kilometers) over steep mountains and across wild rivers. U.S. soldiers had chased these men, women, and children all the way. Their warriors had fought the soldiers, but now most were dead. The army had them trapped. Cold and starving, the Nez Perce could not run or fight.

Chief Joseph did not want his people to suffer any longer. He decided to **surrender**. He turned their weapons over to the U.S. Army. A noble and peaceful man, Chief Joseph earned the respect of his people, white settlers, and U.S. leaders. He is remembered today as a great Native American leader.

Chief Joseph became a symbol of the Nez Perce, their flight to freedom, and their desire for peace.

Several rivers run through the Wallowa Valley. In spring, the Nez Perce fished for salmon. They dried some fish to eat during winter.

Joseph was born in 1840 in the Wallowa Valley of northeastern Oregon. The Nez Perce had lived in the Northwest for hundreds of years. Their land spread over 27,000 square miles (70,000 square kilometers). It also included what are now the states of Idaho and southeastern Washington.

The Nez Perce lived in villages in small groups called **bands**. Each band elected a head chief who represented them in times of peace. Other chiefs planned when and how the band should fight. All the chiefs made decisions together. Joseph's father was a head chief.

The Nez Perce lived in tepees in the summer as they roamed their land. Famous for their horses, the tribe had the largest herd in North America.

Chapter 2

Making Friends and Enemies

The Nez Perce first met white men in 1805 when explorers Meriwether Lewis and William Clark traveled through their land. The Nez Perce were friendly and traded with them and the white settlers who came later.

More white settlers moved to the Northwest. In 1855, the governor of the area made an agreement, or **treaty**, with the Nez Perce. The Indians had to give up some of their land but were allowed to keep a large area for themselves. This land was called a **reservation**.

This painting from 1855 shows the Nez Perce arriving for the treaty meeting with Governor Isaac Stevens.

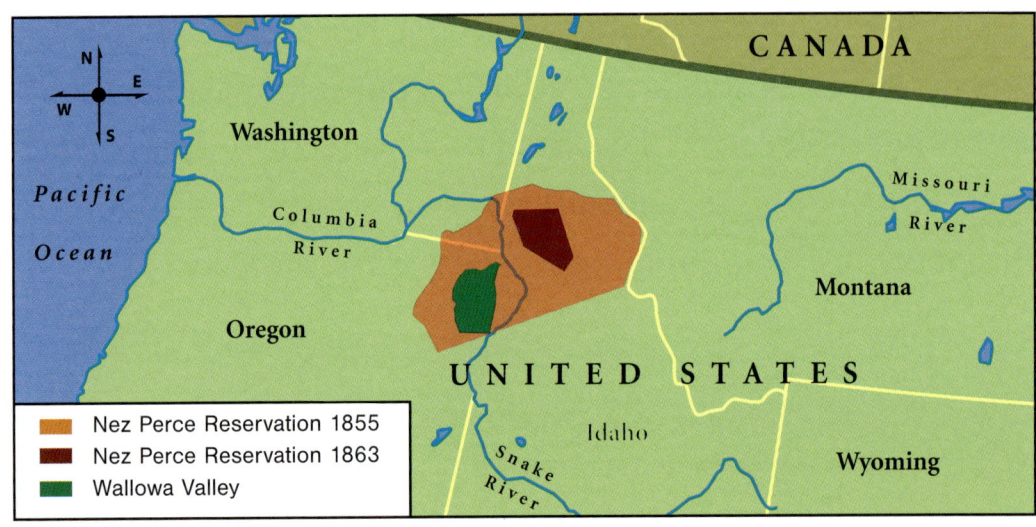

A new treaty in 1863 greatly reduced the size of the Nez Perce reservation. It no longer included the Wallowa Valley.

In 1860, gold was discovered on the Nez Perce reservation. Thousands of miners and settlers flooded onto Nez Perce land. The governor wrote a new treaty. It took away most of the Nez Perce's remaining land. It gave them a tiny reservation in Idaho. Some chiefs signed this treaty. Chief Joseph's father and other chiefs in the Wallowa Valley, however, refused to leave their homeland.

Chapter 3

Leading His People

Joseph became head chief in 1871 when his father died. Joseph believed in solving problems by talking. In May 1877, however, the army said that if the Nez Perce did not leave the Wallowa Valley, it would attack them. Talking with the whites would no longer help. Joseph knew they had to move.

Chief Joseph (*front center*) and his warriors led their people to Idaho. U.S. soldiers attacked them there in White Bird Canyon.

    Some warriors were angry about having to give up their land. They killed a few settlers. Chief Joseph knew that war with the white people would start soon. Joseph, about 250 warriors, and 500 women and children left quickly for Idaho.

    About one hundred soldiers followed them and attacked. The Nez Perce warriors killed many soldiers.

Joseph decided to ask the Crow Indians for help. He led the Nez Perce over the Rocky Mountains toward the Crow's land. The Nez Perce hoped the U.S. Army would not follow them. While they were sleeping, however, the soldiers began shooting. Many Nez Perce were killed, including about fifty women and children.

These tepee poles in Big Hole, Montana, mark the place where the army killed sleeping Nez Perce women and children.

The dotted red line on the map shows the trail Chief Joseph took as he led his people toward safety in Canada.

When the Crow Indians refused to help the Nez Perce, Chief Joseph and the other chiefs decided to go to Canada. It was hundreds of miles away! They would be safe there because the U.S. Army could not enter another country.

About five thousand soldiers now followed the Nez Perce. The war chiefs and warriors hid in the mountains and attacked the army from behind. They kept the soldiers from catching the Nez Perce. The army officers were amazed that so few warriors could hold off all their men.

General Oliver Howard and his soldiers chased the Nez Perce over steep mountain paths.

By late September, the Nez Perce had reached Bear Paw, Montana. Canada was only about 40 miles (64 km) away. The group was tired, cold, and hungry, and many had died. Chief Joseph decided they should rest.

On September 30, the soldiers attacked again. After five days of fierce fighting, Chief Joseph knew that his people could not win or escape.

Ollukut was a warrior and Chief Joseph's brother. He was killed at Bear Paw.

On October 5, 1877, Chief Joseph surrendered. He said, "I am tired of fighting. Our chiefs are killed. It is cold and we have no blankets. The little children are freezing to death. My heart is sick and sad."

When Chief Joseph turned over his weapon, he said, "I will fight no more forever." His surrender speech is one of the most famous statements by a Native American.

Chapter 4

A Statesman for the Nez Perce

Chief Joseph and rest of his band became prisoners of the United States. They had to march hundreds of miles to a reservation in Oklahoma. The weather there was very hot and made many Nez Perce sick. They did not have medicine or clean water. Many of the children and old people died.

When Chief Joseph surrendered, the army had promised that his people could return to their homeland. Two years later, they were still on the Oklahoma reservation. Joseph was sad about the broken promise. He continued to fight for his people's right to go home.

Chief Joseph and his family posed for this photograph in about 1878 while being held prisoners.

In 1879, Chief Joseph traveled to Washington, D.C. He met with the president and other leaders. Joseph understood that his people would not be allowed to return to their Wallowa Valley. Could they live somewhere else in the Northwest? he asked. He also wanted Native Americans to have the same laws as white men. They should be free to travel, work, and trade where they wanted.

Besides Chief Joseph, other groups of Nez Perce also met with government leaders in Washington, D.C.

In 1885, the Nez Perce in Oklahoma were finally sent back to the Northwest. Some went to live in Idaho. Joseph and the warriors went to a reservation in Washington.

On September 21, 1904, Chief Joseph died on the reservation. He is remembered today as a hero of the Nez Perce and a leader for peace.

Chief Joseph was never allowed to return to his home in the Wallowa Valley. When Joseph died, a doctor said it was from a broken heart.

Glossary

bands — groups of Native Americans who live together and elect a chief and other leaders

Congress — the part of the United States government that makes laws

governor — a person who is chosen to govern a colony or territory

homeland — the country or area in which a person was born or has lived a long time

noble — describes someone who is brave, honest, puts the needs of others first, and has good values

represented — acted in place of or for another person or a group

reservation — an area of land that the government sets aside for a special purpose. In the past, Native Americans were assigned, moved, or restricted to reservations. In Canada, these areas are called reserves.

surrender — to admit defeat and give oneself up to an enemy

treaty — an agreement among nations or peoples

For More Information

Books

Chief Joseph. Native American Legends (series). Don McLeese (Rourke Publishing)

Chief Joseph: Nez Perce Peacekeeper. Famous Native Americans (series). Diane Shaughnessy and Jack Carpenter (Rosen Publishing)

Chief Joseph of the Nez Perce. Photo-Illustrated Biographies (series). Bill McAuliffe (Capstone Press)

The Nez Perce Tribe. Native Peoples (series). Allison Lassieur (Capstone Press)

Web Site

The West — Good Words
www.pbs.org/weta/thewest/program/episodes/six/goodwords.htm
Read about the Nez Perce's struggle with white settlers and the U.S. Army in Chief Joseph's own words.

Publisher's note to educators and parents: Our editors have carefully reviewed this Web site to ensure that it is suitable for children. Many Web sites change frequently, however, and we cannot guarantee that a site's future contents will continue to meet our high standards of quality and educational value. Be advised that children should be closely supervised whenever they access the Internet.

Index

armies 4, 5, 11, 13, 14, 15, 19

Canada 14, 16
chiefs 5, 7, 10, 11, 14, 15
children 4, 12, 13, 17, 18
Crow Indians 13, 14

fighting 4, 7, 16, 17

gold 10
governors 9, 10

horses 7

Idaho 6, 10, 12, 21

laws 20
Lewis and Clark 8

Montana 13, 16
mountains 4, 15, 19

Oklahoma 18, 19, 21
Oregon 6

presidents 20
prisoners 18

reservations 9, 10, 18, 19, 21
rivers 4

settlers 5, 8, 9, 10, 12
soldiers 4, 12, 13, 15, 16
speeches 17
surrender 4, 17, 19

treaties 9, 10

Wallowa Valley 6, 10, 11, 20, 21
warriors 4, 12, 15, 21
Washington 6, 21

About the Author

Barbara Kiely Miller is an editor and writer of educational books for children. She has a degree in creative writing from the University of Wisconsin–Milwaukee. Barbara lives in Shorewood, Wisconsin, with her husband and their two cats Ruby and Sophie. When she is not writing or reading books, Barbara enjoys photography, bicycling, and gardening.